Tatting Patterns

Tatting
Patterns

LYN MORTON

GUILD OF MASTER CRAFTSMAN PUBLICATIONS

First published 2002 by
Guild of Master Craftsman Publications Ltd,
166 High Street, Lewes,
East Sussex BN7 1XU

Reprinted 2003

Photographs by Anthony Bailey
Illustrations by Lyn Morton

ISBN 1 86108 261 4

British Cataloguing in Publication Data
A catalogue record of this book is available from the British Library.

Book and cover design by Paul Griffin

Typeface: Garamond

Colour separation by Viscan Graphics Pte Ltd (Singapore)

Printed and bound in Hong Kong by CT Printing Ltd

Contents

A selection of tatting shuttles and hooks

Introduction

IT IS WIDELY BELIEVED that tatting evolved from knotting, an ancient Chinese art. Tatting has also been found as an embellishment on ceremonial burial garments in tombs in Egypt. However, the first recorded reference to tatting is in a poem called *The Royal Knotter*, which was written by Sir Charles Sedley in 1707.

In 1848 Mlle Eleonore Riego de la Branchardière, the daughter of an Irish mother and French father, started to teach new tatting methods and these are thought to be the foundation of the lace as we know it today. Eleonore became quite famous and is thought to have produced the first books of patterns and instructions.

When tatting became popular, it was found that it could be made with a needle, or even on fingers, so it wasn't just the province of wealthy ladies with beautiful shuttles. For this reason it became known as 'poor man's lace' or 'beggar's lace', not because it was inferior, but because it was available to even the poorest needleworker.

Over the years methods have evolved and ingenious new ways of improving the art continue to be found. Designers throughout the world share new ideas and uses and so constantly further the art of tatting. Modern teaching methods and instructions have helped to make tatting an even more accessible and thriving craft and this very old lace form presents many ideas for decorative uses in the modern home.

You will find a great variety of projects in this book, for various skill levels. My aim is to inspire tatters who have a reasonable degree of competence but who do not design for themselves, as well as to provide new ideas for the more experienced tatter. Some of the more simple designs (such as 'Marjorie', on page 16) could be made by a relative beginner, while others (such as 'Emma', on page 32) are more complicated and will appeal to those with greater expertise. But skill levels are not definitive and you, as a tatter, will know instinctively if a particular pattern is within your capabilities.

I hope that you enjoy this book and that it will encourage you to experiment with this wonderful craft.

NOTE
The thread measurements for the patterns in this book are a guide only and refer to the Turkish threads which Lyn normally uses (see 'About the Author', page 106). If different threads are used, the quantities needed may vary slightly.

ABBREVIATIONS USED

DS = Double Stitch	LP = Large Picot
P = Picot	RW = Reverse Work
Sep = Separated by	SP = Small Picot

Patterns/Motifs

Many of the patterns in this section – such as 'Marjorie', 'Snowflake' and 'Meg' – are very simple to make, so are particularly suitable for the less experienced tatter. The other patterns range from fairly simple to those such as 'Sally' and 'Emma', which need a little more practice.

Many of the motifs can be joined together to make larger items, like mats or coasters, and round motif patterns can be stitched onto craft bangles to make hanging decorations.

Pansy Edging

Ring No. 1. Ring of 5DS, 3Ps separated by 5DS, 5DS close. RW chain No. 1. 3DS, P, 7DS, P, 7DS, P, 3DS.

*RW Ring No. 2. Ring of 5LPs and 4SPs worked alternately, separated by 1DS, close. Turn chain No. 2, chain of 8DS, join to the 3rd P of ring No.1, 8DS join to the 1st SP of ring No. 2 chain No. 3, 8DS, P, 8DS join to 2nd SP of ring No. 2, chain No. 4, 8DS, P, 8DS join to 3rd smaller P of ring No. 2 chain No. 5, 8DS, P, 8DS join to 4th small P of ring No. 2 chain No. 6, 8DS, P,

8DS join to the base of ring No. 2.

Turn, chain No. 7, 3DS join to 3rd P of chain No. 1 7DS, P, 7DS, P, 3DS.

RW ring No. 3. 5DS join to the P of chain No. 6 (the last chain of the pansy flower), 5DS, P, 5DS, P, 5DS close. RW chain No. 8 3DS join to the last P of chain No. 7, 7DS, P, 7DS, P, 3DS.*

Work the pattern from * to * to the length required.

Handkerchief with Pansy Edging

Pansy Edging

**Numbers of stitches required for
Pansy Edging**

Five-point Snowflake Motif

Middle flower

Wind the shuttle with only eight turns and leave attached to the ball thread. Make a ring of 5LPs and 4SPs worked alternately, close ring. RW chain of 8DS, P, 8DS join to the first SP of centre ring. Continue round until five petals are completed. Cut and tie into the base of the first petal.

Enlarged centre flower

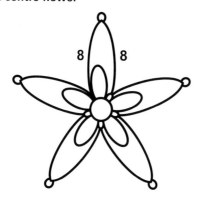

Enlarged middle flower

First Row

Wind shuttle 40 turns. Do **not** cut from ball.

Ring 1. Ring of 6DS, P, 4DS, P, 6DS close. RW chain of 6DS, P, 6DS join to a P of the middle flower 6DS, P, 6DS. RW and continue round the middle flower. Join the last chain to the base of ring 1. Cut and tie. (See diagram below.)

Outside Row

Wind shuttle 50 turns. Do **not** cut from ball.

Ring of 5DS, P, 5DS join to the middle of the chain on the last row where the chain of that row was joined to the middle flower, 5DS, P, 5DS close. RW chain of 3DS, 7Ps separated by 2DS, 3DS join to the first P of the ring on the last row, 3DS, P, 3DS join to the second P of the same ring, (continue chain) 3DS, 7Ps separated by 2DS, 3DS, RW. Continue right round all the remaining petals, cut and tie. (See diagram on facing page.)

First row

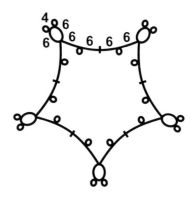

6

The Snowflake Motif is suitable for hanging decorations

Outside row

Six-point Snowflake Motif

The previous five-point flower is suitable for single motifs.

However, if the pattern is needed for something larger, such as a doily, then it would need to be made as a six-point motif.

The middle flower would have six large and five small picots.

The rest of the pattern would be worked to a six point. See the diagram below.

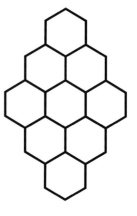

When joined, the Six-point Snowflake is ideal for creating larger items

The Six-point Snowflake Motif

Beads and Picots

Centre Flower

Thread ten beads onto the thread.

Wind the shuttle with 0.5m (approximately 20in) of thread and leave it attached to the ball.

Slide five beads onto the shuttle thread, leaving five beads on the ball thread.

1st ring. Wind the thread round the hand with the beads inside the ring, *work 1DS 1 bead, 1DS, a SP* repeat from * to * four times, 1DS, bead, 1DS, close ring.

RW. Work a chain of six DS, 1SP, 2DS, slide a bead from the ball thread, 2DS, 1SP, 6DS. Join to the first SP of the bead centre. (Join with a shuttle thread to prevent twisting). Continue with the chains in this manner until all five petals are worked. Join the last chain into the base of the first petal, tie and cut.

Second Row

Wind the shuttle with 1m (approximately 3ft) of thread. Leave attached to the ball.

Ring of 1DS, 5LPs separated by 1DS, 1DS close the ring. (DAISY RING) RW, chain of 8DS, join to the second P of a chain on the centre flower, work 3DS then take the chain to the back of the bead, join to the first P of the same chain. Work 8DS. RW.

Repeat from * to * four times. Join the last chain to the base of the first ring. Tie and cut.

Beads and Picots pattern shown as a hanging decoration

Third Row

Wind the shuttle with 1m (approximately 3ft) of thread. Leave attached to ball.

Ring of 5DS, join to the chain behind the bead on the previous row, 5DS close. RW. Chain of 2DS, 15Ps separated by 1DS, 2DS, join to the centre LP of the daisy ring on the second row, (make this join with the shuttle thread), make one LP, 2DS, 15Ps separated by 1DS. RW. Repeat from * to * four times. Join at the base of the first ring. Tie and cut.

Secure all ends well before trimming.

Tudor Rose

Wind the shuttle with 2m (approximately 6ft) of thread, leaving it attached to the ball.

Centre Ring

Ring of one DS 5LP and 4SP worked alternately separated by one DS. Close ring. RW.

First Row of Petals

Chain of one very SP, 8DS, P, 8DS, join to the first SP of the centre ring. Repeat four times. Join the last chain of this row into the SP at the start of the first chain. Do **not** detach but continue the next row of chains as follows:

Second row of petals

One very SP, 10DS, P, 10DS, join to the SP on the base of chain two on the first row of petals.

Repeat this chain around all the petals joining into the SPs on the first row of chain petals. Join the last chain into the SP at the start of the first chain of this second row. Do NOT detach but continue the next row as follows:

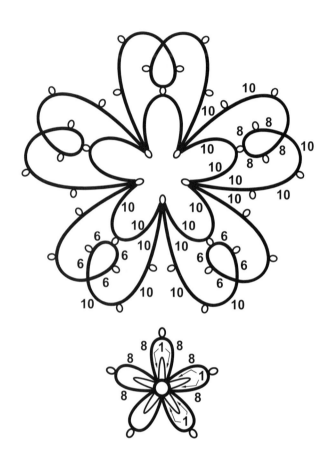

Third Row. Chains and Rings

SP *chain of 10DS, 2Ps separated by 10DS, 10DS. RW, ring of 6DS, P, 6DS, join to the P in the centre of the first chain of the second row, 6DS, P, 6DS, close ring. RW, chain of 10DS, 2Ps separated by 10DS, 10DS. Join to the SP at the start of the second chain of the second row.* Repeat from * to * four times. Join the last chain into the SP at the start of the third row. Tie and cut. Secure ends well before trimming.

Tudor Rose is a lovely decoration for a 5.5cm (2½in) craft bangle

Elegance

If this pattern is worked in Turkish thread it will fit a 7cm (2¾in) diameter ring.

Centre Flower. Ball and Shuttle

Wind approximately 1.5m (5ft) of thread on the shuttle, but leave it attached to the ball. Ring of 7DS, 1LP, 7DS, close ring. RW, *Chain of 7DS, 3Ps separated by 2DS, 7DS. RW. Ring of 7DS. Join to the LP of the first ring, 7DS close ring.* Repeat from * to * five times. RW chain of 7DS, 3Ps separated by 2DS 7DS. Join to the base of the first chain. Tie and cut.

Outer Row. Two Shuttles

Shuttle No. 1: wind with 2.5m (approximately 8ft) of thread. Unwind 3m (approximately 9ft) of thread from the ball and wind it on shuttle No. 2 towards shuttle No. 1.

*Shuttle No. 1: ring of 6DS, join to the third P of chain on centre flower, 6DS, close ring. Start the next ring right up to the first ring. 6DS join to the first P of the next chain of the centre flower, 6DS close ring. RW (still using shuttle No. 1) chain of 8DS, 3Ps separated by 2DS, 8DS. RW. Ring of 7DS join to the centre P of the same chain on the centre

flower, 7DS, close ring. RW. Take up shuttle No. 2. Make a ring of 7DS, P, 7DS, close ring. RW, with shuttle No. 1 work chain as before, (8DS, 3Ps separated by 2DS, 8DS, RW.)* Repeat from * to * five more times. Join the last chain to the base of the first chain where it meets the double rings. Tie and cut. Secure all ends well before trimming.

Elegance – ideal for a coaster

Marjorie

Ball and Shuttle

Wind the shuttle with 2m (approximately 6ft) of thread, leaving it attached to the ball.

Ring one. of 3DS, 2Ps separated by 3DS, 3DS, 1LP, 3DS, 2Ps separated by 3DS, 3DS, close ring.

RW. Chain one. One very SP, 3DS, 7Ps separated by 2DS, 3DS. RW.

Ring two. *3DS, 2Ps separated by 3DS, 3DS, join to the LP of ring one, 3DS, 2Ps separated by 3DS, 3DS close ring. RW, chain as chain 1*. Repeat from * to * four times. Join the sixth chain into the very SP at the start of chain one.

Middle Picot Chains

One very SP, 3DS, 15Ps separated by 2DS, 3DS, join to the SP at the start of the second chain of the last row. Repeat from * to * round all the petals, join the last chain into the very SP at the start of the first chain on this row. (See diagram below).

Outer Picot Chains

One very SP, *3DS, 19Ps separated by 2DS, 3DS, join into the SP at the start of the second chain of the middle row.* Repeat from * to * working round all the petals of the middle row. Join the sixth chain into the very SP at the start of the outer row. (See diagram below.)

Tie and cut. Secure all ends well before trimming.

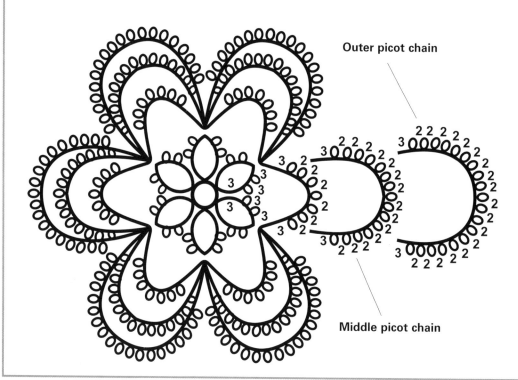

Outer picot chain

Middle picot chain

Marjorie in metallic thread, for a Christmas hanger

Marjorie in cotton thread

Flat Flower Motif (Water Lily)

If this pattern is worked in Turkish thread it will fit into a 6.5cm (2½in) diameter ring. It can also be worked onto a metal ten-point centre instead of working the tatted centre flower. A metal centre would not be practical if you intend to do the raised centre flower (see pattern for this on page 20).

Centre Flower

Wind the shuttle with 1m (approximately 3ft) of thread. Leave attached to the ball. Ring of 1DS, 10LPs and 9SPs, worked alternately separated by 1DS, 1DS, close ring. RW, one very SP, chain of 6DS, P, 6DS, join to the first SP of the ring. Continue with the chains until all the petals are worked, joining the chains into the SPs in between the large ones. When all ten petals are worked join the last chain into the very SP at the start of the first chain. Tie and cut.

Outer row

Centre row

The Flat Flower Motif on its own makes an attractive coaster or hanging decoration

First Outer Row

Wind the shuttle with 3.5m (approximately 11ft) of thread, leaving it attached to the ball.

Ring of 2DS, 2Ps separated by 2DS, 2DS, join to the P on a point of the centre flower, 2DS, 8Ps separated by 2DS, 2DS, close ring. RW, one very SP, chain of 3DS, 9Ps separated by 2DS, 3DS. Join to the fifth P of the ring. RW. Repeat from * to * eight times. TENTH RING. Ring of 2DS, 2Ps separated by 2DS, 2DS, join to the remaining point on the centre flower, 2DS, 2Ps separated by 2DS, 2DS. Join to the first ring of the circle at the very SP at the start of the first chain, 2DS, 5Ps separated by 2DS, 2DS close ring.

TENTH CHAIN. 3DS, 9Ps separated by 2DS, 3DS, join to the very SP at the start of the first chain of this outer row. **Do not cut.** Now continue just working chains as follows:

Second Outer Row

One very SP. *Chain of 3DS, 13Ps separated by 2DS, 3DS, join to the end of the first chain on the last row*. Continue round all the petals in the same way until all the petals are worked. Join into the very SP at the start of the first chain. Tie and cut. Secure all ends.

Water Lily

Raised Centre Flower

Wind the shuttle with 0.5m (approximately 20in) of thread, leaving it attached to ball.

Make a daisy ring of 6LPs and 5SPs worked alternately and close ring. Reverse work, chain of 7DS, P, 7DS, join to the first SP of ring. Continue making the chains until all six petals are completed, then join the last chain into the base of the first chain, cut and tie.

Outer Ring

Wind the shuttle with 3m (approximately 9ft) of thread and leave attached to the ball.

First Ring of 7DS, join to a P of the centre flower, 7DS, 8Ps separated by 2DS, close. RW, Chain of 2DS, 11Ps separated by 2DS, 2DS, join to the first P of ring. RW, ring No. 2 as previous ring, and chain as previous chain. Continue until ring No. 6, ring of 7DS, join to petal of centre flower as before, 7DS, join to the base of first ring, 2DS, 7Ps separated by 2DS, 2DS, close ring. RW, chain as before. Join into base of first ring and chain, cut and tie.

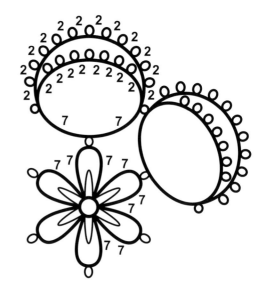

Water Lily pattern showing raised centre flower.
Suitable for a stick-pin brooch or buttonhole flower

Alexandra

Ball and Shuttle

CENTRE MOTIF

Wind the shuttle with 4m (approximately 12ft) of thread, leaving it attached to the ball.

First Trefoil

Ring No.1, ring of 3DS, 5Ps separated by 3DS, 3DS, close ring. *Ring No.2, 3DS, join to the last P on ring 1, 3DS, 8Ps separated by 3DS, 3DS, close ring. Ring No. 3, 3DS, join to the last P of ring No.2, 3DS, 4Ps separated by 3DS, 3DS, close ring.

RW. One very SP, chain of 3DS, 5Ps separated by 3DS, 3DS.

RW. Second Trefoil, Ring No.1, 3DS, 2Ps separated by 3DS, 3DS, join to the centre P of ring No. 3 of the first trefoil, 3DS, 2Ps separated by 3DS, 3DS, close ring.* Repeat from * to * four times. Then repeat ring two. Ring No. 3 on sixth trefoil, ring of 3DS, join to the last P of the last ring, 3DS, P, 3DS, join to the third P of ring No. 1 on the frst trefoil, 3DS, 2Ps separated by 3DS, 3DS, close ring.

RW. Chain as before, join into the very SP at the start of the first. chain. Tie and cut.

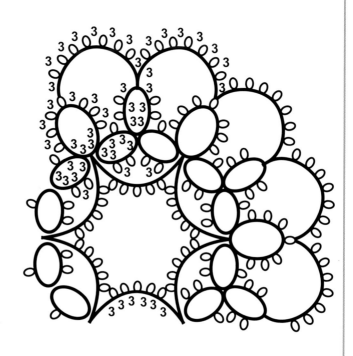

Second Row

Ball and Shuttle. Wind the shuttle with 2m (approximately 6ft) of thread, leaving it attached to the ball. *Ring No.1, 3DS, 2Ps separated by 3DS, 3DS, join to the centre motif at the point where small rings of the trefoils are joined, 3DS, 2Ps separated by 3DS, 3DS, close ring. RW. one very SP. Chain of 3DS, 7Ps separated by 3DS, 3DS. Join to the fourth P of the large ring of the trefoil. Continue chain of 3DS, 7Ps separated by 3DS.* Repeat from * to * five times (but only make the very SP on chain one). At the end of the last chain, join into the very SP at the start of the first chain. Tie and cut. Make sure all ends are secure before trimming.

Alexandra

Joined to make a mat

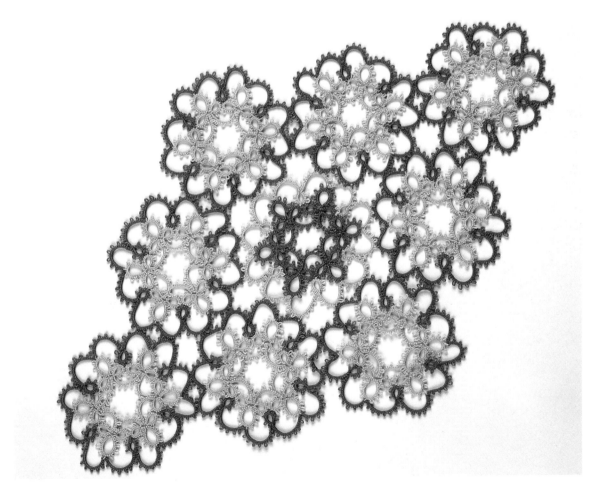

Sophie

Ball and Shuttle

This pattern is worked in one piece. Wind the shuttle with at least 4m (approximately 12ft) of thread, leaving it attached to the ball.

Start with the centre ring of 1DS, 9Ps separated by 1DS, 1DS, close ring. RW, chain of one very SP, 8DS, 1P, 8DS, join to the second P of the inner ring, continue chain as before, joining into alternate Ps of the inner ring, join the fifth petal into the very SP at the start of the first chain. TURN and continue chain of 10DS,** RW* SMALL RING of 8DS, P, 4DS, P, 4DS, close ring. RW and start the next chain 'THE PICOT CHAIN' as near as possible to the base of the ring and the end of the last chain – chain of 2DS, 9Ps separated by 2DS, 2DS, join to the first P of the *SMALL RING.

Continue chain by working 10DS, join to the SP at the point where the last chain of ten started on the middle flower, turn and continue chain of 10DS, join to the same P on *small ring. RW, ring of 7DS, join to the P at the top of the petal on the middle flower, 7DS, 2Ps separated by 7DS, 7DS, close ring. Work chain as previous picot chain, join to the second P of the last ring, continue chain of 10DS, join to the SP at the start of petal (No. 2) on the middle flower. Turn and continue chain of 10DS, join to the centre P of the previous ring.** REPEAT from ** to ** three times, working round the middle flower. Then repeat as far as the last large ring – Ring of 7DS, join to the P on the last free petal of the middle flower, seven DS, join to the base of the first *small ring, 7DS, P, 7DS, close ring. RW, repeat picot chain, join into the same P at the base of the *small ring.

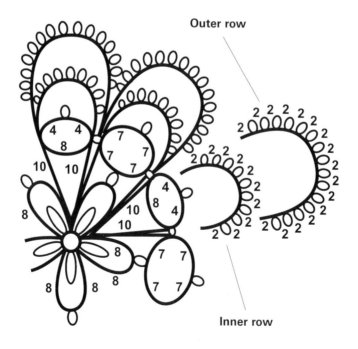

Outer row

Inner row

Sophie, a pattern originally designed for a dream catcher

Outer Row

Now continue with chains only as follows: chain of
3DS, 15Ps separated by 2DS, 3DS join into space at
the P of ring* and continue round all the pattern in this
manner. After the last join, work in further chain of
10DS. Take this down to the bottom of the first chain
of 10DS and secure to the starting point of that chain.
Tie and cut. Secure all ends well before trimming.

Sally

Two Shuttles

Wind Shuttle 1 with 3m (approximately 9ft) of thread, unwind another 3m (9ft) from the ball leaving it attached to shuttle 1, tie the free end to shuttle 2 and wind it towards shuttle 1.

Flower 1

Start with Shuttle 1: daisy ring of 1DS, 5LPs and 4SPs separated by 1DS, 1DS, close ring. RW, one very SP to start *chain of 8DS, picot, 8DS. Join to the first SP of daisy ring.* Repeat the chain four times joining into the SPs round the daisy ring. The last chain joins to the base of the ring. TURN and now with Shuttle 2, start a centre chain of 10DS. Take up Shuttle 1 and make a ring of 2DS, 3Ps separated by 2DS, 2DS, close ring. Back to Shuttle 2 continue chain, 10DS, RW.

Flower 2

Work the Daisy ring and flower as flower one but with Shuttle 2.

Join the last chain to the base of the flower and change to Shuttle 1. Turn and chain 10DS. Shuttle 2 ring of 2DS, 3Ps separated by 2DS, 2DS, close ring. Shuttle 1, chain of 10DS, RW.

Flower 3

Repeat Flower 1. Then with Shuttle 2 chain of 10DS. Shuttle 1 ring of 2DS, P, 2DS, join to the centre P of small ring on the middle of the previous centre chain, 2DS, P, 2DS, close ring.

Shuttle 2 continue chain of 10DS.

Flower 4

Work as Flower 2 with Shuttle 2. Then with Shuttle 1 turn to make chain of 10DS, with Shuttle 2 make a ring of 2DS, P, 2DS, join to the centre P of the small ring in the middle of centre chain 1, 2DS, P, 2DS, close ring, back to Shuttle I, chain of 10DS. Join to the start of chain 1, at the base of Flower 1.

Tie and cut.

Sally, a design using two shuttles

Outer Row

Ball and Shuttle. Wind the Shuttle with 2m (6ft) of thread, leaving the thread attached to the ball.

Ring of 3DS, P, 3DS, join to the first P of chain 1 of Flower 1, 3DS, P, 3DS, close ring. RW, one very SP. Then chain of 3DS, five Ps separated by 2DS, 3DS, join to the P on the second petal of Flower 1. Repeat chain and join to petal 3, and repeat again and join to petal 4, repeat chain again then RW and make a ring of 3DS, P, 3DS, join to petal 5, 3DS, P, 3DS, close ring. Repeat from * to * round Flowers 2, 3 and 4, join to the start of the first chain on Flower 1. Tie and cut.

Secure all ends firmly before trimming.

Ten-flower Oval

First Flower

Thread five beads onto the thread. Wind 0.5m (approximately 20 inches) of thread onto the shuttle and leave it attached to the ball. Keep the beads on the shuttle side of the thread. Put the beads into the circle of thread round the hand for the inner ring of *1DS, slide one bead up to the stitch, 1DS, SP.* Repeat from * to * three times, 1DS, bead, 1DS, close ring. RW, make a very SP **then make a chain of 7DS, P, 7DS, join to the first SP of inner ring between the beads.** Repeat from ** to ** four times. Join the chain into the very SP at the start of the first chain. Tie and cut. Secure firmly before trimming.

Second Flower

Work as for the First Flower but instead of a P, on the last chain join to a P of the First Flower.

Third Flower

Work the Third Flower as before, but this time join to the First Flower at the P to the right of where you joined the Second Flower.

Fourth Flower

Work the flower as before but now join chain one to the Second Flower (see diagram above right), and chain two to the Third Flower.

Fifth to Ninth Flowers

Work these in the same way as the fourth flower, following round the two centre flowers.

Tenth Flower

Work as before but now join the chain to the Third, First and Ninth Flowers.

Make sure all the ends are secure before trimming.

Stitch to the oval craft bangle by all the outside picots.

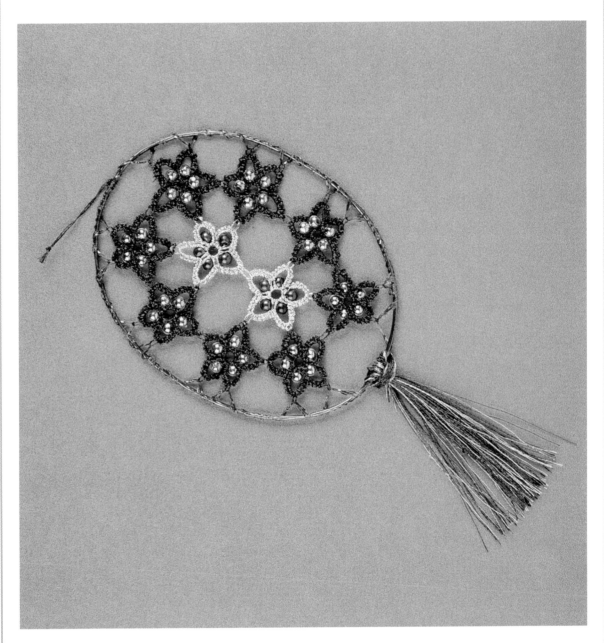

Ten-flower Oval, shown here in an oval craft bangle

Meg

Ball and Shuttle

An alternative to the tatted centre flower could be a six-point metallic centre.

Tatted Centre Flower

Wind the shuttle with 0.5m (approximately 20 inches) of thread and leave the thread attached to the ball.

Daisy ring of 1DS, 6LPs and 5SPs worked alternately, separated by 1DS, 1DS, close ring. RW, 1 very SP, chain of 8DS, P, 8DS, join to the first SP of the daisy ring, continue chains around the daisy ring in this way, join the last chain to the very SP at the start of the first chain. Tie and cut.

Second Row

Ball and Shuttle, wind the shuttle with 1m (approximately 3ft) of thread, leaving the thread attached to the ball. *Ring of 5DS, P, (or bead), 5DS, join to a P on the chain of the centre flower, 5DS, P (or bead), 5DS, close ring. RW, one very SP, chain of 2DS, 11Ps separated by 2DS, 2DS. RW.* Repeat from * to * five times. (Only work the very SP at the start of chain one.) When all the chains have been worked, join into the very SP at the start of chain one. Tie and cut.

Third Row

Ball and Shuttle: wind the shuttle with 2m (approximately 6ft) of thread, leaving it attached to the ball. *Ring No. 1: 6DS, join to the centre P of the chain on the second row, 6DS, close ring. RW, one very SP, chain of 2DS, 7Ps separated by 2DS, 2DS. RW. Ring 2: Ring of 3DS, P, 3DS, join to the tenth P of the chain used to join previous ring, 5DS, close ring. Ring 3: 5DS, join to the second P of the next chain of row 2. 3DS, P, 3DS, close ring. RW. Chain of 2DS, 7Ps separated by 2DS, 2DS, RW.* Repeat from * to * five times. Join the last chain to the very SP at the start of chain one of this row. Tie and cut.

Secure all ends well before trimming.

Meg, made into a window hanger

The Main Pattern 'Emma'

MAIN PATTERN

The Main Pattern comprises several individual patterns or elements and these are identified in the multi-coloured layout shown on the facing page.

The elements may be used individually to make attractive designs or in combination with one, two or three of the other elements to make a range of designs.

The make-up of the elements along with the range of designs is covered in the following pages.

i) Coaster or Centre for Main Pattern shown in scarlet:

ii) The Basic Cross shown in blue:

iii) Triangle Motif shown in pink:

iv) Linking Triangle and Trefoil Edging shown in green:

The Collar

COLLAR PATTERN

As with the Main Pattern, the Collar design comprises the individual patterns shown in the multi-coloured layout on the facing page.

The make-up of the respective design elements, as shown on the facing page, is covered on pages 38, 40 and 43.

THE ELEMENTS

i) The Basic Cross shown as blue

ii) Triangle Motif shown as pink

iii) Linking Triangle and Trefoil Edging shown as green

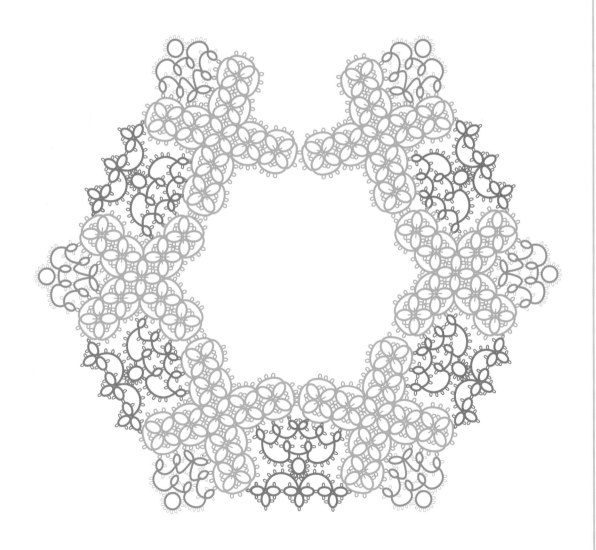

Coaster or Centre for Main Pattern

Wind the shuttle with 1m (approximately 3ft) of thread. Leave the thread attached to the ball.

Ring No. 1. 1DS. 11Ps separated by 1DS. 1DS close. (Daisy Ring).

RW Chain No.1. *1 very SP, 8DS, P, 8DS, join to the second P of ring.* Continue from * to * five times joining into alternate picots of the Daisy Ring. Join the last chain into the very SP at the start of chain 1. Continue chain of * 12DS, P, 4DS. Join to the P at the top of the petal on the centre flower. 4DS, P, 12DS. Join into the very SP at the start of the next chain on the centre flower*. Repeat round all the petals joining the last chain into the base of the first. Cut and tie.

Now wind the shuttle with 3m (approximately 9ft) of thread and leave attached to the ball.

Ring of 5DS, P, 5DS. Join to the P at the top of a petal of the centre flower. 5DS, P, 5DS close. RW. Chain of 5DS. 3Ps separated by 5DS, 5DS, RW. Continue round all the petals in this way. Join the last chain into the base of the first. Cut and tie.

TREFOIL ROW

First Trefoil

*Ring No. 1. 5DS. 3Ps separated by 5DS, 5 DS, close.

Ring No. 2. 5DS. Join to the 3rd P of last ring.
5DS. Join to the centre P of a chain on the previous
round 5DS, P. 5DS. Close.

Ring No. 3. 5DS. Join to the last P of ring 2, 5DS.
LP, 5DS, P, 5DS. Close.

RW. Chain of 5DS. 5Ps separated by 5DS.

Repeat from * until the last Trefoil. When working
Ring 3 of the last trefoil, 5DS. Join into the last P
of Ring 2 as before 5DS. Join to the centre P of
Ring No.1 of the first Trefoil. 5DS, P, 5DS. Close.

RW work the last chain as before. Join to the start
of the first chain and Trefoil. Tie and cut.

Secure all ends well before trimming.

Basic Cross Pattern

The Starting Trefoil

Ring No. 1: 5DS, 3Ps separated by 5DS, 5DS close ring.

Ring No. 2: as Ring No. 1.

Ring No. 3: as Ring No. 1.

RW. Chain of 3DS, 3Ps separated by 3DS, 3DS. All the chains on the basic cross are made this way and will now be referred to only as a chain.

RW. Ring No. 4. 5DS, P, 5DS, join to the centre P of the last ring (No. 3), 5DS, P, 5DS. Close ring.

Ring No. 5, as Ring No. 1. RW. Chain. RW.

Ring No. 6, as Ring No. 4. RW. Chain. RW, Ring No. 7, 5DS, P, 5DS. Join at the point where Rings 5 and 6 are joined, 5DS, P, 5DS, close ring. RW. Chain. Ring No. 8 as Ring No. 7. Ring No. 9, 5DS, P, 5DS, join to the point where Rings Nos. 3 and 4 meet, 5DS, P, 5DS, close ring. RW. Chain.

Ring No. 10 as Ring No. 9.

Ring No. 11: 5DS, P, 5DS, join to the centre P of Ring No. 2, 5DS, P, 5DS, close ring. **Repeat twice from Ring No. 3.**

Fourth Arm of the Basic Cross

Ring No. 3: 5DS, P, 5DS, join to the centre P of Ring No. 1 (on the first arm of the cross). 5DS, P, 5DS, close ring.

Continue in pattern until Ring No. 9 is worked.

Final Chain: work as before. Then join into the base of the very first chain, at the point where Rings Nos. 1, 2 and 3 meet. Secure ends well before trimming.

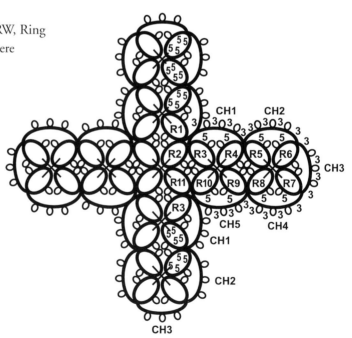

Basic Cross in metallic thread

The Basic Cross joins to
the Main Pattern Coaster
at positions 'A' to 'L'

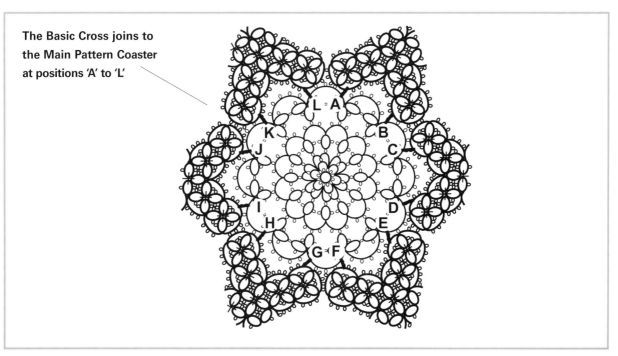

TRIANGLE MOTIF ALONE

Two Shuttles

Wind Shuttle 1 with 2m (approximately 6ft) of thread. Shuttle 2 with 1.5m (5ft).

Using Shuttle No. 1, Ring No. 1, 3DS, 3Ps separated by 3DS, 3DS, close.

RW Chain No. 1. 4DS, P, 4DS, P, 4DS.

RW Ring No. 2 as Ring No.1.

RW Chain No. 2 as Chain 1.

RW Ring Nos. 3 and 4 as Ring No.1.

RW Chain No. 3 as Chain No.1.

RW Ring No. 5 as Ring No.1.

RW Chain No. 4 as Chain No.1.

RW Ring No. 6 as Ring No.1.

TURN and change to Shuttle No.2.

Chain No. 5 of 5DS, 6Ps separated by 3DS, 5DS. RW.

Ring No. 7, 3 DS, P, 3DS, join to the first worked P of Chain No. 3. 3DS, P, 3DS, close. RW.

Chain No. 6, small chain of 5DS.

Change to Shuttle No. 1. Ring No. 8. 5DS, join to the last P of Chain No. 5, 3DS, 9Ps* separated by 2DS, 3DS, P, 5DS, close.

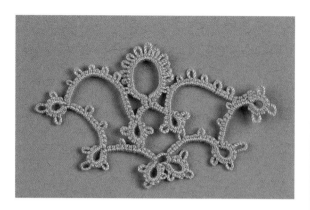

Change to Shuttle No. 2. Chain No. 7. Small chain of 5DS. RW: Ring No. 9: 3DS, join to the second P of Chain No. 2, 3DS, P, 3DS, close.

RW Chain No. 8, 5DS, join to the last P of the large ring, 3DS, 5Ps separated by 3DS, 5DS.

Join to the base of the first ring. Secure all ends well before trimming.

*The Large Ring can have 9Ps or 11Ps when working this pattern.

TRIANGLE MOTIF FILL-IN FOR THE BASIC CROSS PATTERN

Two Shuttles

Shuttle 1: wind 2m (approximately 6ft).
Shuttle 2: wind 1.25m (approximately 4ft).

Ring No. 1. Shuttle No. 1, 3DS, P, 3DS, join to the first P of the first side chain of the Basic Cross, 3DS, P, 3DS, close.

RW Chain No. 1, 4DS, P, 4DS, P, 4DS.

RW Ring No. 2, 3DS, P, 3DS, join to the 3rd P of the same chain as before of BC. 3DS, P, 3DS, close.

RW Chain No. 2 as Chain No. 1.

RW Ring No. 3. 3DS, P, 3DS, join to the first P of the next chain of BC. 3DS, P, 3DS, close.

Ring No. 4. 3DS, P, 3DS, join to the third P of the next chain of BC. 3DS, P, 3DS, close.

RW Chain No. 3 as Chain No. 1.

RW Ring No. 5. 3DS, P, 3DS, join to the first P of the next chain of BC. 3DS, P, 3DS, close.

RW Chain No. 4 as Chain No. 1.

RW Ring No. 6. 3DS, P, 3DS, join to the last P of side chain of the Basic Cross, 3DS, P, 3DS, close.

TURN and change to Shuttle No. 2.

Chain No. 5 of 5DS, 6Ps separated by 3DS, 5DS.

RW Ring No. 7. 3DS, P, 3DS, join to the first P of Chain No. 3, 3DS, P, 3DS, close.

RW Chain No. 6 of 5DS.

Change to Shuttle No. 1. Ring No. 8. 5DS, join to the last P of the large chain. 3DS, 9Ps separated by 2DS, 3DS, P, 5DS close. Change to Shuttle No. 2. Chain No. 7 of 5DS.

RW Ring No. 9. 3DS, P, 3DS, join to the second P of Chain No. 2, 3DS, P, 3DS, close.

RW Chain No. 8. 5DS, join to the last P of the large ring continue chain 3DS, 5Ps separated by 3DS, 5DS.

Join to the base of the first ring of the triangle. Secure all ends well before trimming.

THE LINKING TRIANGLE

Two Shuttles

Wind Shuttle No. 1 with 2m (approximately 6ft) of thread. Leave attached to the ball thread and unwind a further 1.5m (approximately 5ft). Wind this onto Shuttle No. 2.

Shuttle No. 1.

Ring No. 1. 3DS, P, 3DS, join to the centre P on the chain of the joining arm of the Basic Cross (BC). See Join 'A' on the diagram on the facing page. 3DS, P, 3DS, close.

RW Chain No. 1. 4DS, 2Ps separated by 4DS, 4DS.

RW Ring No. 2. 3DS, P, 3DS, join to the first P on the next chain of BC (Join 'B' – see diagram on facing page). 3DS, P, 3DS, close.

RW Chain No. 2. As Chain No.1.

RW Ring No. 3. 3DS, P, 3DS, join to the 3rd P of chain on BC. (Join 'C') 3DS, P, 3DS, close.

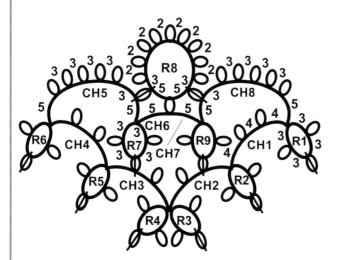

Ring No. 4. 3DS, P, 3DS, join to the first P of next chain on BC. (Join 'D') 3DS, P, 3DS, close.

RW Chain No. 3 as Chain No. 1.

RW Ring No. 5. 3DS, P, 3DS, join to the third P of the same chain of BC. (Join 'E') 3DS, P, 3DS, close.

RW Chain No. 4 as Chain No. 1.

RW Ring No. 6. 3DS, P, 3DS, join to the centre P of the next chain on BC (Join 'F'). 3DS, P, 3DS, close. TURN and change to Shuttle No. 2.

Chain No. 5. 5DS, join to the first P on the last side chain of the BC. (Join 'G') 3DS, 6Ps separated by 3DS, 5DS.

RW Ring No. 7. 3DS, P, 3DS, join to the first P of

Chain No. 3 of triangle (Join 'H') 3DS, P, 3DS, close.

RW Chain No. 6. 5DS.

Change to Shuttle No. 1 for Ring No. 8. 5DS, join to the last P of Chain No. 5 (Join 'I') 3DS, 9Ps separated by 2DS, 3DS, P, 5DS, close.

Change to Shuttle No. 2. Chain No. 7. 5DS.

RW Ring No. 9. 3DS, P, 3DS, join to the second P of Chain No. 2 (Join 'J') 3DS, P, 3DS, close.

RW Chain No. 8. 5DS, join to the first P of the large ring (Join 'K') 5Ps separated by 3DS, 3DS, join to the third P of BC (Join 'L') 5DS, join to the base of Ring No. 1 of Linking Triangle (Join 'M').

Secure all ends well before trimming.

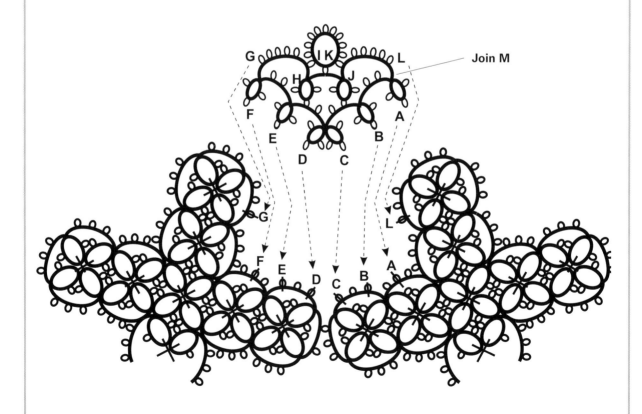

TREFOIL FINISH TO LINKING TRIANGLE

First Trefoil

Ring No. 1. 5DS, P, 5DS, join to the first P on the end section of the BC. 5DS, P, 5DS, close.

Ring No. 2. 5DS, join to the last P of the previous ring. 5DS, P, 5DS, P, 5DS, close.

Ring No. 3 as Ring No. 2.

RW Chain of 3DS. 4Ps separated by 3DS, 3DS, join to the third free P on the large ring of the Linking Triangle. 3DS, P, 3DS.

RW Second Trefoil. Ring No. 1. 5DS, P, 5DS, join to the centre P of the last ring of First Trefoil 5DS, P, 5DS, close.

2nd and 3rd Rings as First Trefoil.

RW Chain 3DS, P, 3DS, join to the fourth P from the last join to the large ring. 3DS, 4Ps separated by 3DS, 3DS.

RW Third Trefoil. Ring No. 1 of 5DS, P, 5DS, join to the centre P of the last ring on the Second Trefoil. 5DS, P. 5DS, close.

Ring No. 2 as in First Trefoil.

Ring No. 3. 5DS, join to the last P of Ring No. 2. 5DS, join to the last P of the end chain of the BC. 5DS, P, 5DS, close.

Secure ends well before trimming.

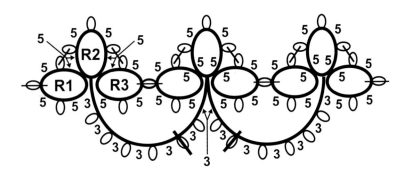

Rings = R
Chain = CH

THREE TRIANGLE MOTIFS JOINED TO MAKE A COASTER

As this coaster matches the Main Pattern (see page 33) it makes an attractive alternative to the usual dressing table set

NOTE: This ring can have 9 or 11 Picots for this pattern

The pattern 'Emma' (see page 32)

Traditional Cross

For this Cross, use the Basic Cross Pattern on page 38 but extend one arm, as shown in the diagram below. Instead of turning round at Chain No. 3 continue for two more patterns and turn at Chain No. 5.

A larger cross can easily be worked by doubling all stitch instruction numbers.

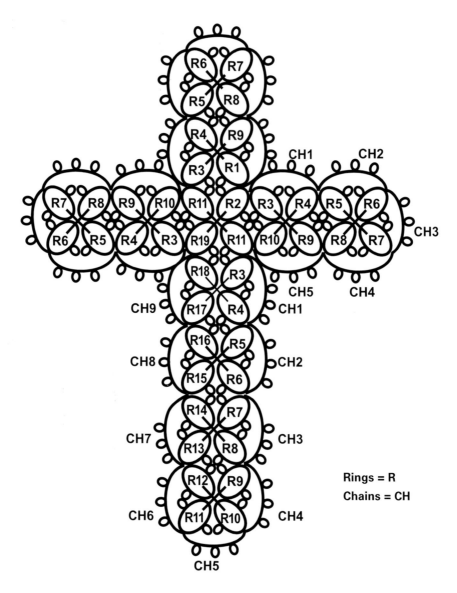

Rings = R
Chains = CH

Traditional Cross bookmark

Fan

Make and join four Basic Cross Patterns (page 38) with linking triangles, as for the Main Pattern.

For the end trefoil shuttle only, wind the shuttle with 0.75m (approximately 30in) of thread.

Ring No. 1. 3DS, P, 3DS, P, 3DS, join to the centre P of end chain on arm of Basic Cross (BC). 3DS, P, 3DS, P, 3DS, close.

Ring No. 2. 3DS, P, 3DS, P, 3DS, join to the last P on next chain of BC. 3DS, join to the first P on the next chain of BC. 3DS, P, 3DS, P, 3DS, close.

Ring No. 3. 3DS, P, 3DS, P, 3DS, join to the centre P of the last side chain of BC. 3DS, P, 3DS, P, 3DS, close. Tie and Cut.

The trefoil edge on the linking triangle is optional.

Mount the lace on net and secure to the fan sticks.

Detail of end trefoil

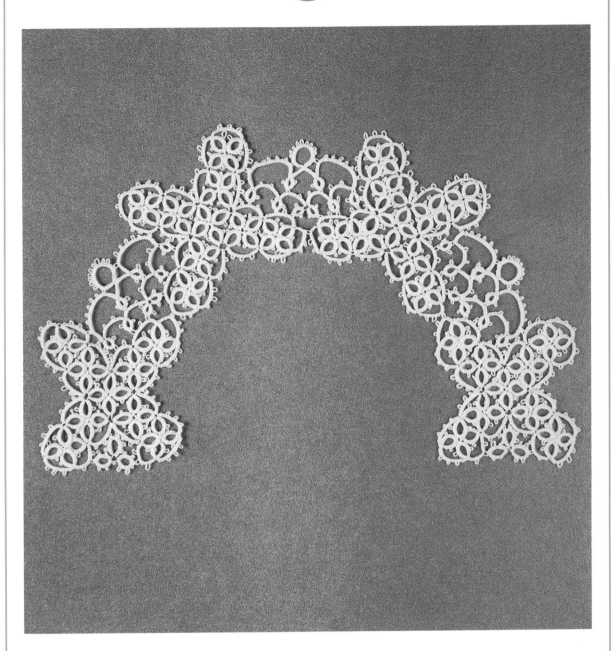

This pattern is suitable for attaching to fan sticks

Lisa

Wind the shuttle with 0.5m (approximately 20in) of thread and leave it attached to the ball.

For centre flower: ring of 1DS, 4LPs and 3SPs worked alternatively and separated by 1DS, 1DS close ring.

RW, Chain of 1 very SP, 10DS, P, 10DS, join to the first SP of the centre flower. Continue chains like that round the four petals joining the end of the last chain into the very SP at the start of the first chain.

Continue chain for the outer row thus: 1 very SP, chain of 15DS, P, 5DS join to the P at the top of the first petal on the last row, 5DS, P, 15DS join into the very SP between the first and second petals. Continue chain of 15DS, P, etc. (On the outer row you only need to make a very SP on the first outer chain). Continue round all the four petals and join the last chain into the very SP at the start of the first outer chain. Secure ends well before trimming.

A number of these small motifs can be joined together to make a garland or an edging. If joined into a square or a diamond shape it is suitable for a doily. The motif when first worked needs to be pressed flat or fingered into shape. I use the Turkish 50 thread (slightly finer than the UK 20) if it is for something like a doily, but I use the Turkish 70 if it is for a handkerchief edging. For details of joins see Diagram 'A' below and 'B' on facing page.

Diagram A

A diamond-shaped mat made with the pattern Lisa

Diagram B

Motif for a Pop-over Collar

Wind the shuttle with 1.5m (approximately 5ft) of thread, leave attached to the ball.

*Ring No. 1. 5DS, 3Ps separated by 5DS, 5DS close. RW.

Chain No. 1. 4DS, 5Ps separated by 4DS, 4DS. Join to the first P of ring No. 1.

Chain No. 2 as chain 1. Join to the centre P of ring No.1.

Chain No. 3. 4DS. RW.

Ring No. 2. 3DS. 3Ps separated by 3DS. 3DS close. RW.

Chain No. 4. 4DS.* The diagram on the right shows how to JOIN the CENTRE RINGS .

Repeat from * to * 3 times. Join the last small chain of 4DS to the base of chain No.1.

To join the motif together, work as far as chain No. 10, 4DS, P, 4DS, P, 4DS. Join to the centre P of chain No. 5 of the previous motif, 4DS, P, 4DS, P, 4DS.

At chain No. 13, 4DS, P, 4DS, P, 4DS. Join to the centre P of chain No. 2 of previous motif. 4DS, P, 4DS, P, 4DS.

Finish as for first motif.

The collar can be made to various sizes by adding or omitting the number of motifs.

This motif also makes up into a doily or coaster. See Diagrams 'A', 'B' and 'C' overleaf.

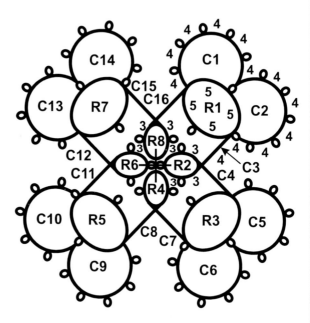

Rings = R

Chains = C

Pop-over Collar (diagrams for this shown on page 54)

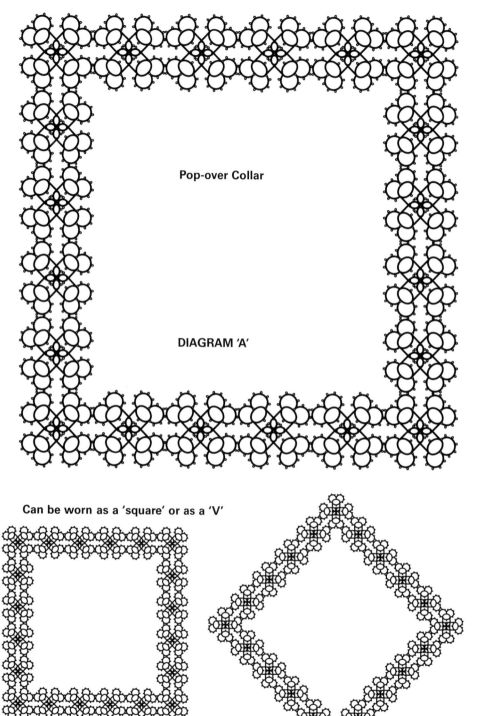

Pop-over Collar

DIAGRAM 'A'

Can be worn as a 'square' or as a 'V'

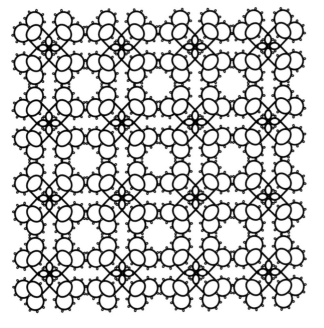

DIAGRAM 'B'

This motif makes a good square shape for a mat or runner or, when worked corner to corner, a diamond shape as shown in Diagram 'C' below

A single row makes an edging or blouse-front trim

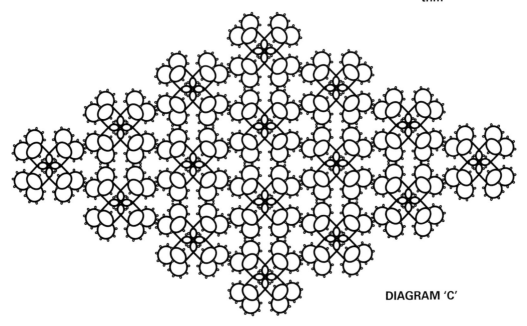

DIAGRAM 'C'

Jewellery and Accessories

The patterns in this section are mainly in the middle-skill range. The 'Black Choker Necklace', for instance, needs some knowledge of the split-ring technique.

Earrings for Pierced Ears

Thread five beads onto thread, then wind the shuttle with 0.25m (approximately 10in) thread, keeping the beads on the shuttle side of the thread.

Put the beads into the circle of thread round the hand for the inner ring of *1DS, bead, 1DS, SP,* repeat from * to * three times, 1DS bead 1DS close. RW chain of 4DS, SP, 4DS, join to the first P of ring, continue round all the beads. When the five petals have been made, tie into the base of the first chain.

This completes the small earring (as shown in the diagram on the right). Now simply place the pin-type earring through the middle.

For a larger earring (as shown below and on the facing page) do not cut the thread when the first round of petals has been made: continue round again, but this time each petal has 6DS, P, 6DS and joins are made into the same P of the ring as before.

Different effects can be achieved by adding more picots to the chains, or by making the chains larger.

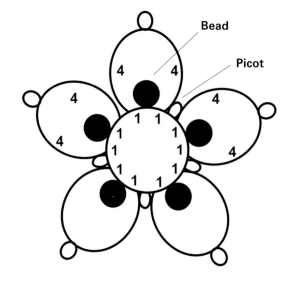

Tatted earring

Collar 'Eunice'

First Row

Wind the shuttle fully and leave attached to the ball.

Ring of 2DS, 7Ps, separated by 2DS, 2DS close. RW Chain of 4DS, 3Ps separated by 2DS, 4DS. RW ring of 2DS, P, 2DS join to sixth P of previous ring 2DS, 5Ps separated by 2DS, 2DS close.

Work to length required for collar. Chains should be of even numbers, for example two chains for each complete pattern.

Second Row

Wind shuttle fully and leave attached to ball. *Ring 1 of 6DS, P, 6DS close. RW chain of 6DS join to the centre P of the first chain of row 1. 6DS, P, 8DS. RW ring of 6DS join to P of ring 1 6DS close. Ring of 5DS, P, 5DS, P, 5DS close. RW chain of 8DS.

RW Trefoil

Ring of 5DS, join to second P of previous ring 2DS, 4Ps separated by 2DS, 5DS close. Ring of 5DS, join to the last P of previous ring 2DS, 6Ps separated by 2DS, 5DS close. Ring of 5DS join to last P of previous ring, 2DS 4Ps sep by 2DS, 5DS close.

RW Chain of 8DS.

RW ring of 5DS join to the last P of previous ring, 5DS, P, 5DS close. Ring of 6DS, P, 6DS close.

RW chain of 8DS join to P of matching chain. 6DS join to the next centre P of row 1, 6DS RW.* Repeat pattern from * to * until last pattern. RW ring of 6DS join to P of previous ring 6DS close.

**The Collar Eunice: one of my first designs, from 40 years ago,
designed for my mother Eunice**

Tudor Rose Stick-pin Brooch

Stick-pin Brooch

Wind shuttle with 0.5m (approximately 20in) of thread and leave it attached to the ball.

Ring of 1DS, 7LPs and 6SPs, worked alternately, separated by 1DS, 1DS close.

Chain of 8DS, 5Ps separated by 2DS, 8DS. Join to first SP of ring. Continue chain of 8DS, join to fifth P of previous chain 2DS, 4Ps separated by 2DS, 8DS join to second SP of centre ring. Continue making chains until all 7 are complete, tie into base of the first chain, cut and secure.

Outside Row

Wind shuttle with 0.5 metre (approximately 20in) of thread, and leave the thread attached to the ball.

Join into previous row between petals and chain 3DS, 5Ps separated by 2DS, 3DS, join into the next point between petals. Continue round in this way until all 7 petals are complete. Join into base of the first outer chain, secure and cut.

Centre Flower

String 5 beads onto thread and, with the thread still attached to the ball, wind 0.5m (approximately 20in) onto the shuttle.

Keeping the beads inside the circle make a ring: 1DS, bead, 1DS, SP. 4 times, 1DS, bead, 1DS, close.

RW chain of 8DS, join to first SP of ring, then continue round every bead until all five chains are complete.

Join into base of the first chain, secure and cut.

Secure the flower to the stick-pin head, with stitches or glue.

The Stick-pin Brooch. As an alternative, the design could be attached to a brooch back

Black Choker Necklace

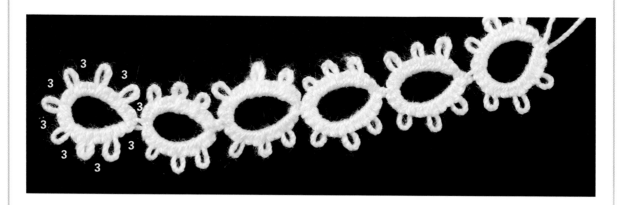

First Row

Row No. 1 is made by a strip of SPLIT RING TATTING.

Wind shuttle No. 1 and leave attached to the ball thread, unwind about 2m (6ft) of thread from the ball and wind onto Shuttle No. 2.

Ring No. 1. Shuttle No. 1, 3DS, 7Ps separated by 3DS, 3DS close. Ring No. 2 (both shuttles) start the split ring method. 1st half 3DS, 3Ps separated by 3DS, 3DS. Second half 3DS, 3Ps separated by 3DS, 3DS close ring. Continue in this way until correct length has been made. Make the last ring as ring No. 1, secure and cut.

Outer Rows

Wind the shuttle and leave it attached to the ball of thread. Ring No. 1, 3DS, 3Ps separated by 3DS, 3DS join to the centre P of ring No. 1, on split ring row, 3DS, 3Ps separated by 3DS, 3DS close. RW chain of 4DS, 3Ps separated by 3DS, 4DS. RW, ring No. 2, 3DS, P, 3DS, join to sixth P of ring 1. 3DS,

P, 3DS, join to the centre P of ring 2 of split ring row. 3DS, 3Ps separated by 3DS, 3DS close.

Continue until end of row, finishing with a ring. 3DS, P, 3DS join to previous ring, 3DS, join to the centre of the last ring of row 1, 3DS 3Ps separated by 3DS close, secure and cut. Complete second side as first.

Thread a fine ribbon through the centre of the split-ring row and tie, or fix, necklace fasteners to each end of the lace.

Choker necklace, using some split ring technique

Gold and Silver
Necklet and Earrings

This article looks really impressive worked in DMC Fil or Clair (art no. 276), which is gold and silver ribbon-like thread. Coats Diadem could also be used.

Necklet

Wind the shuttle fully and leave attached to the ball of thread. Start with ring of 3DS, 3Ps separated by 3DS, 3DS close. RW chain of 4DS, P, 4DS, RW ring of 3DS, join to third P of ring No. 1, 3DS, 2Ps separated by 3DS, 3DS close.

Continue until you have the required length and end with a ring. Cut off and sew in ends.

Flower

Ring No. 1, of 5DS, P, 4DS, P, 4DS, P, 5DS, close. Ring No. 2, 5DS join to the third P of ring 1, 4DS P, 4DS, P, 5DS close.

Rings Nos. 3, 4 and 5 are as ring No. 2.

Ring No. 6, 5DS join to P No. 3 of ring No. 5, 4DS, P, 4DS join to the first P of ring No. 1, 5DS, close.

Earrings

Shuttle only, Ring No. 1 of 6DS, P, 2DS, P, 2DS, P, 6DS close. Ring No. 2, 6DS join to third P of ring No.1, 2DS, P, 2DS, P, 6DS close.

Cut, tie and sew in ends. Attach to earring loop at the point where the two tatted rings are joined.

If you wish beads may be added.

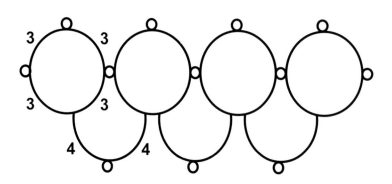

A very simple and elegant design, using metallic, ribbon-like thread

Wedding Hoop

First Row

Wind the shuttle and leave attached to the ball.

Ring of 3DS, 5Ps separated by 3DS, 3DS, LP, 3DS, P, 3DS close. *RW chain of 3DS, 5Ps separated by 3DS, 3DS.

RW ring of 3DS, P, 3DS, join to the LP of the previous ring 3DS, 3Ps separated by 3DS, 3DS large picot 3DS picot, 3DS close.*

Repeat from * to * 19 times then the chain once more, RW ring of 3DS picot 3DS join to the LP of the last ring, 3DS, 5Ps separated by 3DS, 3DS close.

Second Row

String 21 beads onto the ball thread and wind the shuttle with about 2m (6ft) of thread. Leave thread attached to the ball, with the beads on the ball side. Join the thread to the first P of the first chain of row No. 1. Now working chain only for this row – *2DS, 4Ps separated by 2DS, 2DS slide bead down ball thread to meet the stitches already worked, 2DS, 4Ps separated by 2DS, 2DS. Join to the fifth P of the first chain of row No. 1, 3DS join to the first P of second chain on row No. 1*. Repeat from * to * until end of row, finish with the last chain attached to the last picot of chain on row No. 1. Tie and cut. Sew in ends.

Flower

String 18 beads onto the thread. Wind the shuttle with 1m (approximately 3ft) of thread, leaving the thread attached to the ball. Slide 12 of the beads onto the shuttle and leave the other 6 on the ball thread.

1st ring 4DS slide 1 bead from shuttle thread 3DS, LP, 3DS bead 4DS, close.

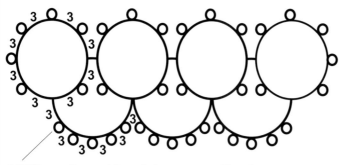

*JOIN: see Second Row below   **First Row**

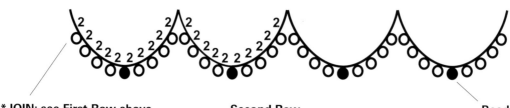

*JOIN: see First Row above   **Second Row**   **Bead**

Wedding hoop

*RW chain of 5DS picot 5DS slide bead from ball thread, 5DS, P, 5DS.

RW ring of 4DS bead 3DS, join to the LP of first ring 3DS bead 4DS close.* Repeat from * to * until six petals are worked.

Cut and tie into the base of the first ring.

User a larger bead to secure the flower to the hoop when stitching into place.

Starch the hoop well. When dry, thread fine ribbon through the rings of row one. Tie in a bow, and stitch to secure.

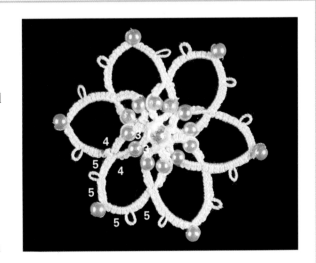

Flower trim

Corsage of Flowers

Six-petal Flower

Centre Flower

Wind the shuttle with 0.5m (20 inches) of thread and leave it attached to the ball.

Make a daisy ring of 6LPs and 5SPs worked alternately and close ring. Reverse work chain of 7DS, P, 7DS, join to the first SP of ring. Continue making the chains until all 6 petals are completed then join the last chain into the base of the first chain, cut and tie.

Outer Ring

Wind the shuttle with 3m (approximately 9ft) of thread and leave it attached to the ball.

1st Ring of 7DS join to a P of the centre flower, 7DS, 8Ps separated by 2DS close. RW Chain of 2DS 11Ps separated by 2DS, 2DS, join to the first P of the ring.

Corsage, showing various sizes of flower

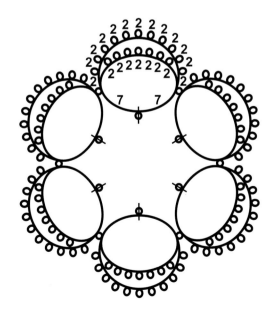

RW 2nd Ring as previous ring, and chain as previous chain. Continue until ring No. 6, ring of 7 DS, join to petal of centre flower as before, 7DS join to the base of 1st ring 2DS, 7Ps separated by 2DS, 2DS close, RW chain as before. Join into base of 1st ring and chain, cut and tie.

Make three flowers for small spray. Make six flowers for corsage

Secure together with florists wire. Trim as desired, e.g. with pearls.

This pattern also works for five-petal flowers. For base daisy make the centre ring of 5LPs and 4SPs.

For a seven-petal flower the base daisy needs 7LPs and 6SPs.

**Corsage of Flowers: a selection of these flowers can be attached to
a headband to make a lovely bridal headdress**

Ring cushion with flower trim

Beaded Butterfly

String 19 beads onto thread.

Wind the shuttle with 1m (approximately 3ft) of thread and leave attached to the ball. Keep the beads on the shuttle.

Ring 1 the centre. Ring of 2DS, 5Ps separated by 2DS, 2DS close. RW chain of 1ODS, RW ring of 3DS, bead, 3DS, bead, 3DS, P, 3DS, bead, 3DS bead, 3DS close. RW chain of 1DS, 18Ps separated by 1DS, 1DS, RW join to P on

beaded ring chain 12DS join to the first P of the centre ring. Turn and chain 12DS, join to the same P of beaded ring as before. RW ring of 1DS, bead, 3DS, bead, 3DS, bead, 3DS, P, 3DS, bead, 3DS, bead, 3DS, close. RW chain of 1DS, 18Ps separated by 1DS, 1DS join to the P on the 5 beaded ring, continue chain of 2DS, 6Ps separated by 2DS, join to the 2nd P of the centre ring.

Chain of 5DS, LP, 3DS, LP, 5DS join to the fourth P of centre ring, continue chain of 2DS, 6Ps separated by 2DS, 2DS. RW ring of 1DS, bead, 3DS, bead, 3DS, bead, 3DS, P, 3DS, bead, 3DS, bead, 3DS, close. RW chain of 1DS, 18Ps sep by 1DS, 1DS join to the P of the previous beaded ring. Chain of 12DS join to P 5 of centre ring, turn chain of 12DS join to the P of the beaded ring, chain of 1DS 18Ps separated by 1DS, 1DS.

RW ring of 3DS bead, 3DS, bead join to the P of the previous beaded ring, 3DS, bead, 3DS, bead, 3DS close. RW chain of 1ODS join to base of centre ring continue chain of 6DS, bead, 6DS join back to the base of the centre ring. Tie and cut.

Tatted Butterfly. Ideal for a dress trim or brooch

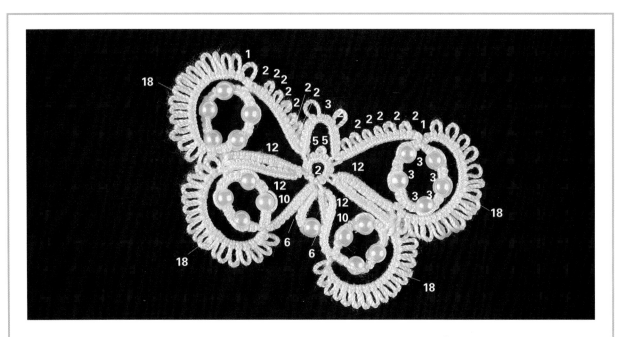

Butterfly, showing the number of stitches required

Greetings Cards

This section contains items for all skill levels.
The pattern 'Simplicity', for instance, on page 90, is
one of the very easy range, while some others are for the
more advanced tatter.

Blank cards can be purchased from card suppliers, craft
shops and some stationers. A good quality, clear glue is
needed to fix the designs to the card.

Although these designs are headed 'Greetings Cards',
the motifs can be used for other items, too: many can
be joined to make such things as mats and, when
stitched onto craft bangles, the round ones make 'dream
catchers', Christmas decorations, or window hangers.

Small Flowers

Ball and Shuttle

For each Flower, wind shuttle with 0.5m (approximately 20 inches) of thread, leaving it attached to the ball.

Flowers No. 1, 2, 3 and 4 start with the same centre Daisy Ring: 1DS, 5LPs and 4SPs, worked alternately, separated by 1DS, 1DS, close ring. Proceed as follows.

Flower No. 1

Flower No. 2

Flower No. 3

Flower No. 1: After daisy ring RW *Chain of 10DS, P, 10DS, join to the first vacant small P of daisy ring.* Repeat from * to * 4 times. Join the last chain into the start of the first chain. Tie and cut.

Flower No. 2: After daisy ring RW. *Chain of 8 DS, P, 5 DS, P, 5 DS, P, 8 DS, join to the first vacant small P of daisy ring*. Repeat from * to * 4 times. Join the last chain into the start of the first chain. Tie and cut.

Flower No. 3: After Daisy Ring RW. *Chain of 17DS. Join to the first vacant small P of daisy ring.* Repeat from * to * 4 times. Join the last chain into the start of the first chain. Tie and cut.

Greeting card trimmed with small flowers

Flower No. 5

Flower No. 4

Flower No. 4: after daisy ring RW. *Chain of 8DS, 5Ps, separated by 2DS, 8DS. Join to the first vacant small P of daisy ring*. Repeat from * to * 4 times. Join the last chain into the start of the first chain. Tie and cut.

Flower No. 5 is a six-ring flower. Shuttle only. Wind the shuttle with 1m (approximately 3ft) of thread.

Ring of 8DS, 3Ps, separated by 5DS, 8DS, close ring. *Start the next ring as near as possible to the base of the previous ring. Ring of 8DS. Join to the last P of previous ring, 5DS, 2Ps, separated by 5DS, 8DS, close.* Repeat from * to * three times. Ring No. 6, 8DS, join to the last ring as before, 5DS, P, 5DS, join to the first P of Ring No. 1, 8DS, close ring. Tie and cut.

Leave ends of thread to form stems if required.

Ring of 1DS, 5 or 7 or 9 LPs separated by 1DS, 1DS, close.

Ring of 1DS, 5LPs and 5SPs worked alternately, separated by 1DS, 1DS, close.

Daisy Rings are a good way to use oddments of various colours and weights of threads. Three variations are shown below.

Variations on the Daisy Rings

Margaret

Centre Flower (6 petals). Ball and Shuttle. Wind the Shuttle with 0.5m (approximately 20 inches) of thread. Leave attached to the ball.

Daisy Ring of 1DS, 6LPs and 5SPs. Worked alternately, separated by 1DS, 1DS, close ring.

RW. 10DS, P, 10DS, join to the first small P on the daisy ring. Turn and work chain petals round the daisy

ring joining into the small Ps, join the last chain into the base of the first chain. Cut and tie.

Flower row. Ball and Shuttle. Now wind the shuttle with 4 metres (about 4½ yards) of thread. Leave attached to the ball.

*Ring No.1, 1DS, 5LPs and 4SPs, worked alternately, separated by 1DS, 1DS, close ring. RW.

Work as the centre flower, making 5 petals instead of 6.

After joining the last petal TURN and continue Centre Chain of 8DS, P, 8DS, join to the P on the end of a petal of the Centre Flower, 8DS, P, 8DS.*

Repeat from * to * 5 more times (round all the petals of the Centre Flower). Join the last centre chain into the start of the first centre chain. Secure all ends well before trimming.

The work will benefit from a light pressing at this point, to keep it flat for the last row to be added.

Outer Row. Ball and Shuttle

Wind the shuttle with approximately 1m (3ft) of thread and leave it attached to the ball.

*Ring No. 1. 6DS, join to the P on the end of the first petal of a flower on the flower row, 3DS, P, 3DS, join to the corresponding petal of the next flower, 6DS, close ring.

RW. Chain of 2DS, 5Ps, separated by 2DS, 2DS. (All the chains on the outer row are the same). Join to the P on the end of the next petal.

Daisy Ring

Centre Flower

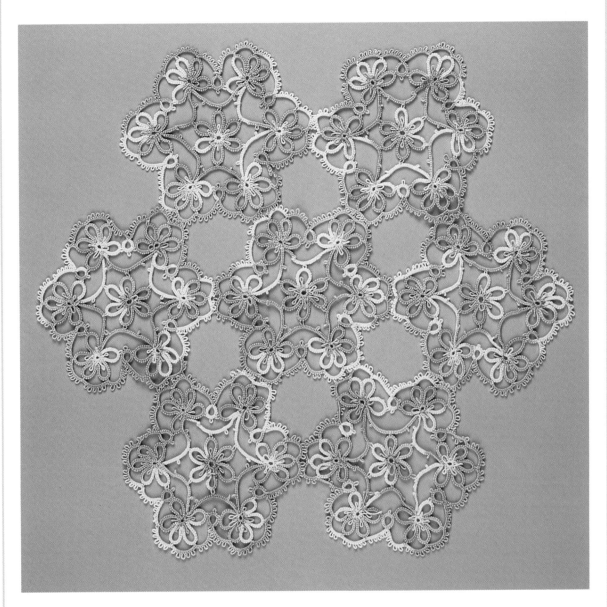

Margaret, joined to make a large mat or table centre

Continue chains, joining to the top Ps, making
4 chains.* Repeat from * to * round all the
Flowers, joining the last chain into the base of
Ring No. 1.

Secure ends well before trimming.

Five-flower version of the pattern 'Margaret'

For this version of the pattern (see the diagrams on
the facing page), the Centre Flower is worked to
only 5 petals, e.g. the small daisy ring is 5LPs and
4SPs worked alternately and then the general
pattern can be followed.

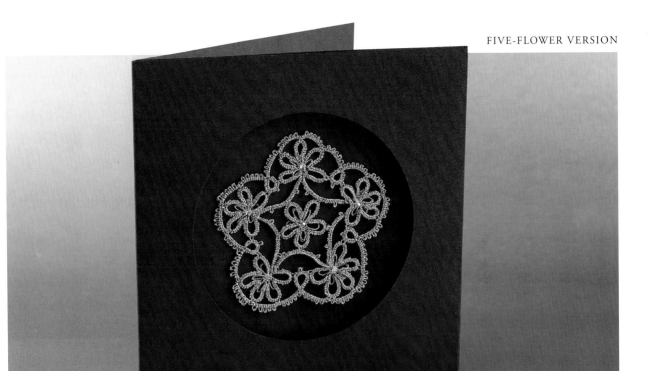

The Centre Flower

The Daisy Ring

Judith

Ball and Shuttle

Wind the shuttle with 2m (approximately 6ft) of thread and leave attached to the ball.

Ring No. 1. 3DS, 3Ps, separated by 3DS, 3DS, close ring.

RW. Small Chain of 5DS.
(NOTE: all Small Chains are of 5DS.)

Ring No. 2. 5DS, 3Ps, separated by 5DS, 5DS, close ring. RW.

Chain 1A: 5DS, 5Ps, separated by 5DS, 5DS, join to the first joining P of Ring No. 2 (see diagram below).

Continue Chain 1B as 1A, making the join to the centre P of the same ring. (2nd joining P) continue chain of 5DS. Ring No. 3, 3DS, P, 3DS, join to the centre P of Ring No. 1, 3DS, P, 3DS, close. RW. Small chain. RW. Ring No. 4, as Ring No. 2.

RW. Chain 2A, 5DS, P, 5DS, join to the corresponding P of Chain 1B. 5DS, 3Ps, separated by 5DS, 5DS, join as for the first joining P and continue chain as for 1B. Join as for the second joining P, continue with a small chain.

RW. Ring No. 5 as Ring No. 3.

RW. Small chain.

RW. Ring No. 6 as Ring No. 2.

RW. Chain 3A, as Chain 2A and 3B as Chain 2B, joining to Ring No. 6. Small chain.

RW. Ring No. 7 as Ring No. 1.

RW. Small chain.

RW. Ring No. 8 as Ring No. 2.

RW. Chain 4A as 2A and 4B as 2B, joining to Ring No. 8. Small chain.

RW. Ring No. 9, 3DS, P, 3DS, join to the centre P of Ring No. 7, 3DS, P, 3DS, close.

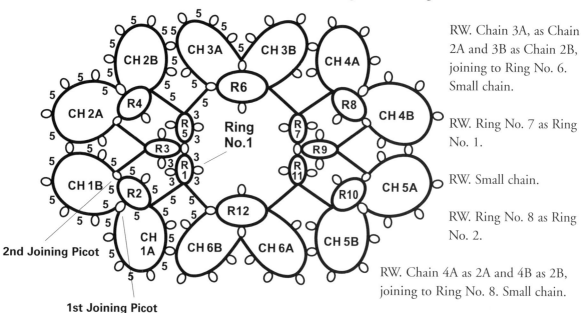

2nd Joining Picot

1st Joining Picot

R = Ring and CH = Chain
*All Small Chains are 5 Double Stitches

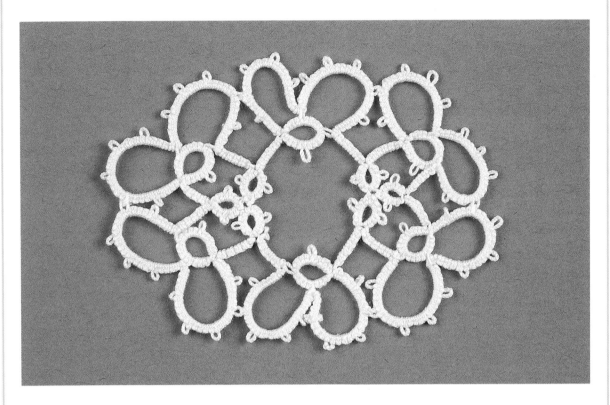

RW. Small chain.

RW. Ring No. 10 as Ring No. 2.

RW. Chain 5A as Chain 2A and 5B as 2B. Joining to Ring No. 10. Small chain.

RW. Ring No. 11 as Ring No. 3.

RW. Small chain.
RW. Ring No. 12 as Ring No. 2.

RW. Chain 6A as 2A and 6B as follows: 5DS, 3Ps, separated by 5DS, 5DS, join to the second P of Chain 1A, 5DS, P, 5DS. Join to the end of P of Ring No. 12, continue chain of 5DS.

Join to the start of the first small chain.

Round

Ball and Shuttle

Wind the shuttle with 1m (approximately 3ft) of thread and leave it attached to the ball.

Ring No. 1. 3DS, 3Ps, separated by 3DS, 3DS close ring.

RW. Small chain of 5DS.
(NOTE: all small chains will be of 5DS).

RW. Ring No. 2. 5DS, 3Ps separated by 5DS, 5DS, close.

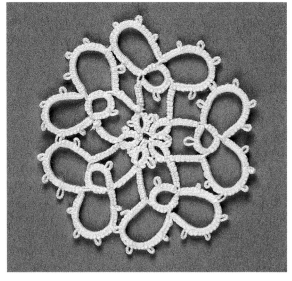

RW. Chain 1A. 5DS, 5Ps separated by 5DS, 5DS. Join to the nearest P on Ring No. 2. Continue Chain 1B as Chain 1A. Join to the end P on Ring No. 2. Continue with a small chain.

RW. Ring No. 3. 3DS, P, 3DS. Join to the centre P of Ring No. 1. 3DS, P, 3DS, close.

RW. Small chain.

RW. Ring No. 4. as Ring No. 2.

RW. Chain 2A, 5DS, P, 5DS, join to corresponding P of Chain No. 1B. 5DS, 3Ps separated by 5DS.

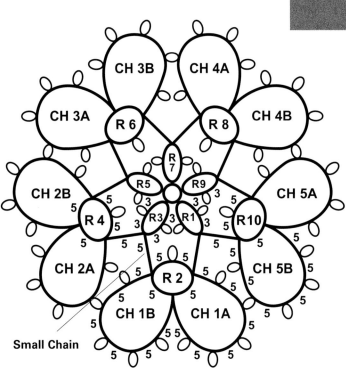

R = Ring and CH = Chain

*All small chains are 5 double stitches

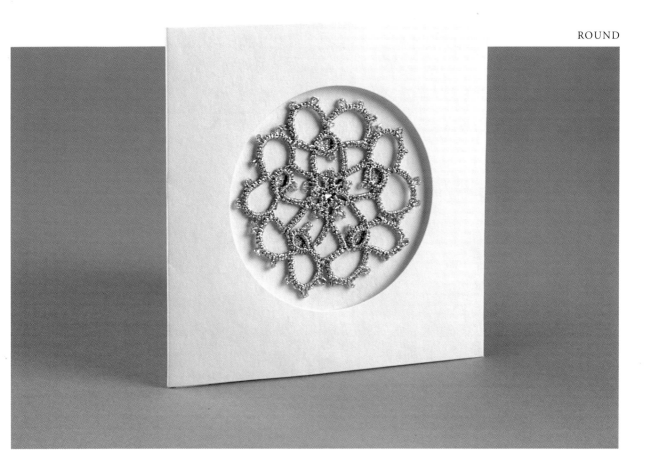

Join to the nearest P on Ring No. 4. Continue Chain 2B as 1B.

Join to the centre P of Ring No. 4. Continue with a small chain.

RW. Ring No. 5 as Ring No. 3.

RW. Small chain.

RW. Ring No. 5 as Ring No. 3.

RW. Small chain.

RW. Ring No. 6 as Ring No. 2.

RW. Chains 3A and 3B are as 2A and 2B. Continue after join with a small chain.

RW. Ring No. 7 as Ring No. 3.

RW. Small chain.

RW. Ring No. 8 as Ring No. 2.

RW. Chains 4A and 4B are as 2A and 2B. Follow after join with a small chain.

RW. Ring No. 10 as Ring No. 2.

RW. Chain 5A as 2A. Chain 5B. 5DS, 3Ps separated by 5DS, 5DS. Join to the corresponding P of Chain IA, 5DS, P, 5DS. Join to the centre P of Ring No. 10. Continue with a small chain. Join to the start of small chain and Ring No. 1.

Cut and secure ends well.

Simplicity

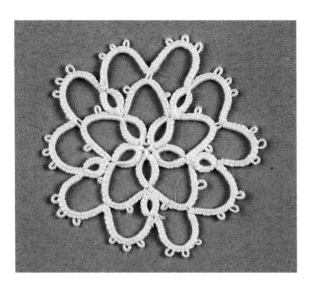

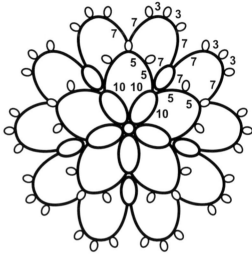

Centre Flower

Ball and Shuttle

Wind the Shuttle with 1m (approximately 3ft) of thread and leave it attached to the ball.

Ring No. 1. 10DS, LP, 10DS, close ring.

*RW. Chain 1, one very SP, 5DS, 3Ps, separated by 5DS, 5DS.

RW. Ring No. 2. 10DS. Join to the large P on Ring No. 1. 10DS, close.*

Repeat from * to * 3 times.

RW. Chain as before. Join to the very SP at the start of Chain 1. Cut and secure ends.

Second Row

Wind the shuttle with 1m (approximately 3ft) of thread and leave attached to ball.

*Ring No. 1. 7DS, join to a chain of the centre flower where it meets a ring, 7DS. Close.

RW. Chain 1A. 7DS, 3Ps, separated by 3DS, 7DS. Join to the centre P of chain of centre flower. Continue Chain 1B as 1A. RW.*

Repeat until the last chain. When that has been worked join into the start of the first chain. Cut and secure ends well.

This simple design looks well with beads added (see facing page). Instead of picots add 40 beads to the ball thread before winding the shuttle. As all the beads will be added to the chains keep them on the ball thread, sliding a bead into position as required.

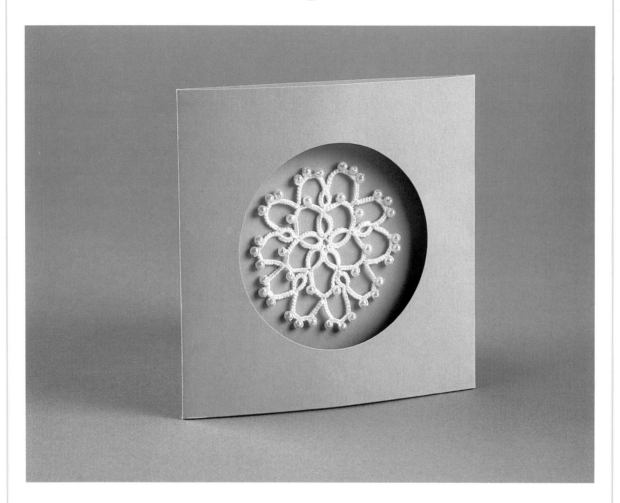

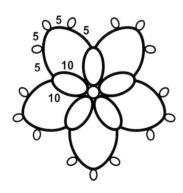

If making a matching gift tag, use the centre flower only

Shamrock

Ball and Shuttle

Wind the Shuttle with 4m (approximately 12ft) of thread and leave it attached to the ball.

First Trefoil

Ring No. 1. 7DS, 3Ps separated by 7DS, 7DS, close ring.

Ring No. 2. 7DS. Join to the last P of Ring No. 1. 7DS, P, 5DS, LP, 5DS, P, 7DS, P, 7DS, close.

Ring No. 3. 7DS, join to the last P of Ring No. 2, 7DS, 2Ps separated by 7DS, 7DS, close.

RW. Chain 1. 5DS, 7Ps, separated by 3DS, 5DS. Join to the end P of Ring No. 3. Repeat Chain 1. RW.

Second Trefoil

Ring of 7DS, P, 7DS, join to the end P of previous ring (Ring No. 3. on 1st Trefoil). 7DS, P, 7DS, close. Ring No. 2, 7DS, join to the last P of Ring No. 1, 7DS, P, 5DS, join to the large P on Ring No. 2 of the 1st Trefoil. 5DS, P, 7DS, P, 7DS, close.

Ring of 7DS, join to the last P of Ring No. 2, 7DS, P, 7DS, P, 7DS, close.

RW. Repeat Chains. RW.

Third Trefoil as Second

RW. Repeat Chains. RW.

Fourth Trefoil

Repeat until 3rd Ring. 7DS, join to the last
P of Ring No. 2, 7DS, join to the centre P of
Ring No. 1 on 1st Trefoil, 7DS, P, 7DS, close.

RW. Repeat Chains. Join the last chain into
the start of the first chain.

Cut and secure ends well.

The space at the top of the card allows you
to add a greeting.

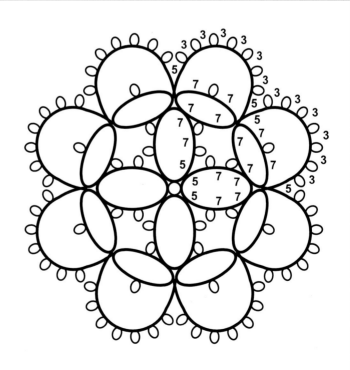

Peggy

**Four-petal Pattern
(Five-petal Pattern on page 96)**

Centre Flower. Ball and Shuttle. Wind the Shuttle with 0.5m (approximately 20in) of thread and leave

it attached to the ball.

Daisy ring of 1DS. Four LPs and three SPs worked alternately, separated by 1DS, 1DS, close ring.

RW. Chain 1. 1 very SP. *7DS, 3Ps, separated by 7DS, 7DS. Join to the first SP of daisy ring.* Repeat from * to * 3 times, joining the chains into the small Ps of the daisy ring. Join the last chain into the very SP at the start of chain No. 1.

Second Row. Ball and Shuttle. Wind the shuttle with 3m (approximately 9ft) of thread and leave it attached to the ball.

Ring No. 1. *7DS, P, 7DS. Join to a P on the end of a petal of the centre flower, 7DS, P, 7DS, close ring.

RW. Chain No. 1, 5DS, 5Ps, separated by 3DS, 5DS.

RW. Ring No. 2, 3DS, P, 3DS. Join to the last P on Ring No. 1, 3DS, P, 3DS, close ring.

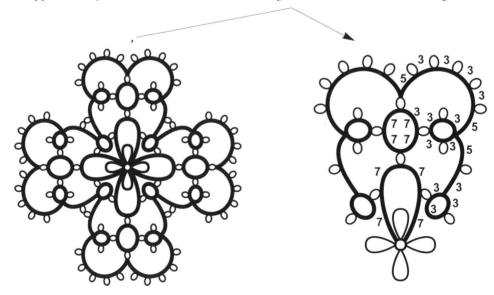

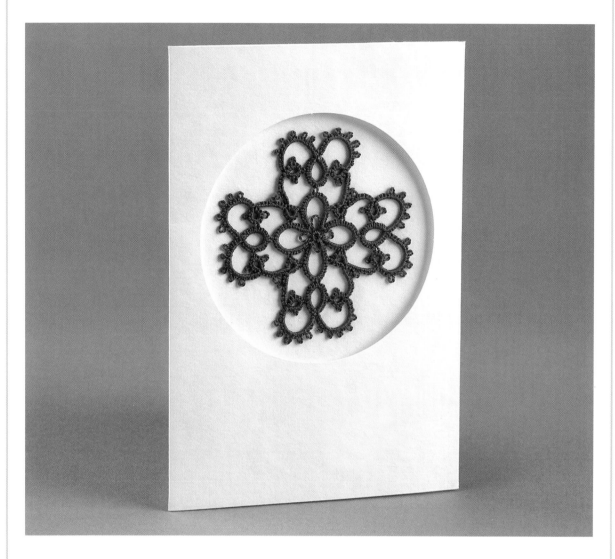

RW. Chain No. 2, 5DS, P, 3DS.

RW. Ring No. 3. Ring of 3DS. Join to the P on the side of the petal of the centre flower. 3DS, join to the side P of the next petal of the centre flower, 3DS, close ring.

RW. Chain No. 3, 3DS, P, 5DS.

RW. Ring No. 4 of 3DS, 3Ps, separated by 3DS, 3DS, close ring.

RW. Chain No. 4. Chain of 5DS, 5Ps, separated by 3DS, 5DS.

RW. Ring No. 5 as Ring No. 1 but join the first P to the end P of Ring No. 4.

RW.* Repeat from * to * three times.

Join the last chain to the start of Chain No. 1.

Five-petal Pattern

For this five-petal version, start with a daisy ring of 5LPs and 4SPs and then follow the pattern for the second row, winding 3.5m (approximately 11ft) of thread and repeating the pattern around all the petals.

**Daisy ring of 5 large picots
and 4 picots alternately**

Rosie

ROSIE 1

Ring No. 1. 7DS, 3Ps, separated by 7DS, 7DS close ring.

RW. 1 very SP, chain of 3DS, 11Ps separated by 2DS, 3DS, join to centre P of ring.

RW. Repeat the Rings and Chains to the desired lengths and then after the last join of chain to ring, join to the very SP at the start of Chain 1.

Cut and tie.

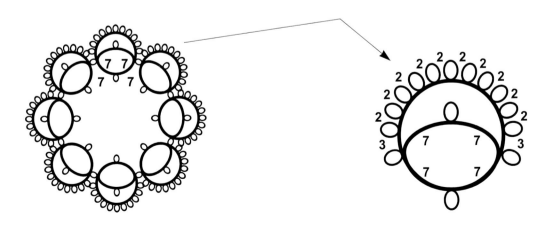

ROSIE 1: a very simple pattern, which is ideal for beginners

ROSIE 2 (see facing page)

After completing Rosie 1 to the required length, join as pattern but do not cut. Instead, TURN and make a row of chains on the inside of the rings thus: chain of 3DS, 5Ps separated by 2DS, 3Ds, join to the centre P of the last ring, where the outer chain was joined. Continue chains in this manner to the end and secure all ends well before trimming.

ROSIE 2: a slightly more advanced pattern

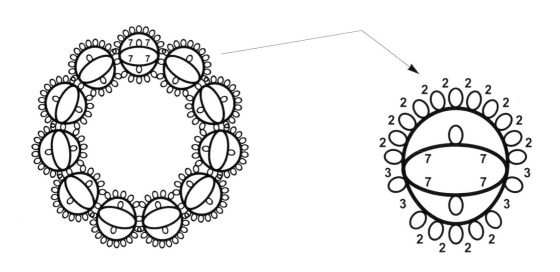

Hearts and Flowers

Hearts and Flowers No.1

Ball and Shuttle. Wind the shuttle with 4m (approximately 12ft) of thread and leave it attached to the ball.

Ring No. 1, Centre Daisy Ring. Ring of 1DS, 6LPs and 5SPs, worked alternately, separated by 1DS, 1DS, close ring.

RW. Chain No. 1, 1 very SP, 9DS.

RW. Ring No. 2, 7DS, 3Ps, separated by 7DS, 7DS, close ring.

RW. Chain No. 2, 9DS, 2Ps, separated by 9DS, 9DS.

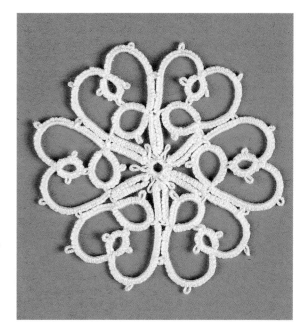

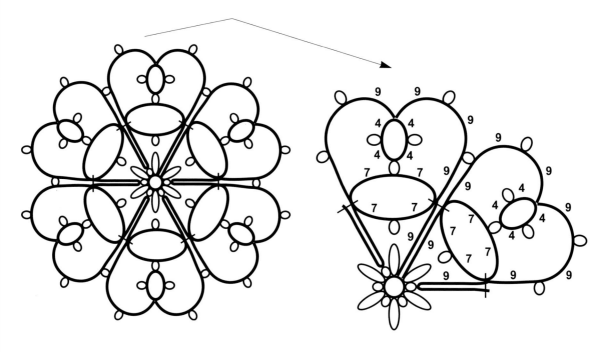

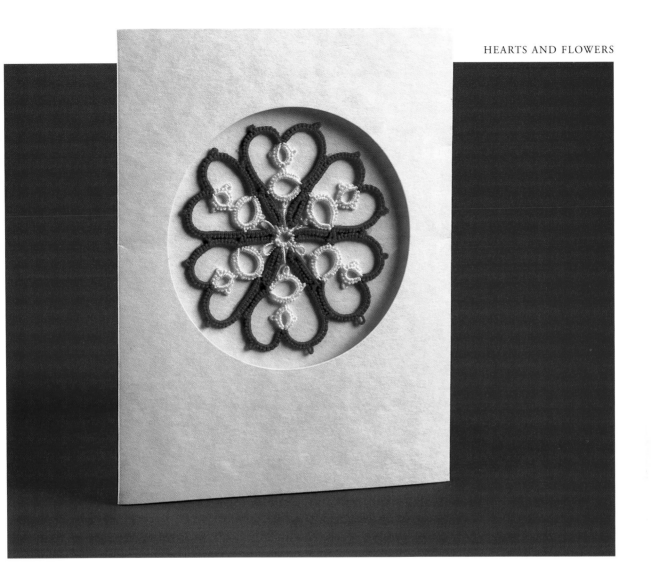

*RW. Ring No. 3, 4DS, P, 4DS, join to the side P, (first) of Ring No. 2, 4DS, P, 4DS, close ring.

RW. Chain No. 3, 9DS, 2Ps, separated by 9DS, 9DS. Join to the centre P of Ring No. 2. Continue chain of 9DS, join to the next SP of daisy ring. Turn and continue chain 9DS. Join to the end of P of Ring No. 2 where Chain 3 also joins.

RW. Ring as Ring No. 2.

RW. Chain of 9DS, join to the side P of Chain 3 on the last petal, 9DS, P, 9DS.*

Repeat from * to * 4 times.

RW. Ring as Ring No. 3.

RW. Chain of 9DS, P, 9DS, join to the first P of Chain 2, 9DS. Join to the end P of last Ring No. 2 and also to the base of the first Ring No. 2.

Continue chain of 9DS, join to the very small P at the start of Chain No. 1.

Cut and tie.

Secure all ends well before trimming.

Hearts and Flowers No. 2

Ball and Shuttle. Wind the shuttle with 5m (approximately 15ft) of thread and leave it attached to the ball.

Ring No. 1, Small Daisy Ring of 1DS, 5SPs, separated by 1DS, 1DS, close ring.

RW. Chain No. 1, 1 very SP, 9DS.

RW. Ring No. 2, 2DS, 11Ps, separated by 2DS, 2DS, close.

RW. Chain No. 2, 9DS, 2Ps, separated by 9DS, 9DS.

*RW. Ring No. 3, 1DS, 7Ps, separated by 1DS, join to the third P on the side of Ring No. 2, 1DS, 7Ps, separated by 1DS, 1DS, close.

RW. Chain No. 3 of 9DS, 2Ps, separated by 9DS, 9DS. Join to the centre P (P No. 6) of Ring No. 2. Continue chain of 9DS, join to the next SP of Ring No. 1 (Daisy Ring). Turn and continue chain 9DS. Join to the end of P of Ring No. 2 where Chain 3 also joins.

RW. Ring as Ring No. 2.

RW. Chain of 9DS, join to the side P of Chain No. 3 on the last petal, 9DS, P, 9DS.*

Repeat from * to * 4 times. RW. Ring as Ring No. 3.

RW. Chain of 9DS, P, 9DS, join to the first P on Chain No. 2 of the first pattern, 9DS. Join to the end P of last Ring No. 2 and also to the base of the first Ring No. 2. Chain 9DS, join to the very SP at the start of Chain No. 1.

Cut and tie. Secure all ends well before trimming.

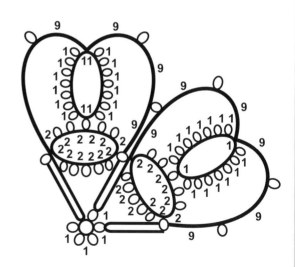

Hearts and Flowers makes an ideal trim for a Valentine card

A Five-point Star

Centre Flower. Ball and Shuttle.

Wind the shuttle with 0.5m (approximately 20 in) of thread and leave it attached to ball.

Start with a Daisy Ring of 1DS, 5LPs and 4SPs worked alternately, separated by 1DS, 1DS, close ring.

RW. Chain of 10DS, P, 10DS. Join to the first small P of daisy ring, continue chains in this way until the last chain has been worked. Join into the start of Chain 1. Secure ends and cut.

Outer Row. 2 Shuttles

Wind Shuttle No. 1 with 2m (approximately 6ft) of thread then unwind a further 3m (approximately 9ft)

from the ball and wind it on shuttle 2 towards Shuttle No. 1.

*Begin with Shuttle No. 1, Ring No. 1, of 10DS, join to the P on the centre of a petal of the centre flower, 10DS, close. Take up Shuttle No. 2, Ring No. 2, 6DS, 3Ps, separated by 2DS, 6DS, close ring.

Chain 1, Shuttle No. 1. Chain of 3DS, 5Ps, separated by 3DS, 3DS. Join to the point between petals of the centre flower, continue with chain of 3DS, 5Ps, separated by 3DS, 3DS. RW.*

Repeat from * to * 4 times. Join the last chain into the point where Rings No. 1 and 2 meet.

Centre Flower

About the Author

Lyn Morton learned to tat about forty years ago, when suffering a long spell in hospital. She became bored with knitting and reading but, from the moment she saw some tatting, was determined to learn the craft. She soon became a proficient tatter and it greatly helped her recovery.

For a number of years raising a family and running a business were Lyn's priorities but, once her two sons had grown up, she renewed her interest in tatting and began to produce a large number of innovative and versatile tatted designs.

Lyn teaches tatting at her workshops and is an enthusiastic member of the Ring of Tatters – the worldwide organisation for the craft – and she continues to demonstrate tatting and promote the Ring whenever possible.

Her company, Tatting and Design has made available to tatters a very wide range of high-quality threads from Turkey, as well as books on tatting. These products are now available to customers worldwide via the company website (http://www.tatting.co.uk).